GWEN STRAUSS

# TRAIL
# STONES

ILLUSTRATED BY ANTHONY BROWNE

ALFRED A. KNOPF

NEW YORK

# INTRODUCTION

I began writing these poems in 1987 at a time when I was exploring the theme of metamorphosis in fairy tales. Anthony Browne heard me read several of them at a symposium at Simmons College. He had also been working with fairy tale themes, but he didn't want, at that stage, to do a book of conventional illustrations. We were both interested in approaching fairy tales from a new perspective. We decided to collaborate on a book in which a combination of drawings and poems would form a collection of portraits, in the hope that such a collection might open a small door into the quieter moments of transformation and reveal those dark and startling events that lie buried within the stories.

A fairy tale read aloud to me when I was a child is not the same as the fairy tale I read again today. There are forgotten details. I forgot, for example, the years Rapunzel's prince wandered blindly; the hazel tree Cinderella planted on her mother's grave; the missing golden plate from Sleeping Beauty's christening feast. Writing these poems from the perspective of different characters, seemingly strange and haphazard objects wanted to be reported: characters demanded certain props, a mirror, a golden ball. In searching for their private voices I discovered private details, the integrity of their objects; and I began to appreciate the depth of their individual stories.

Whether it is a princess calling down a well, a witch seeking out her reflection, children following a trail into the woods, falling asleep or into blindness, a common thread in our portraits is that each of these characters is compelled to turn inward. Though each confronts different issues – fear of love, shame, grief, jealousy, loneliness, joy – they have in common a time of solitude. They are enclosed within a private crisis. They have entered a dark wood where they must either face themselves, or refuse to, but they are given the choice to change. The momentum of self-revelation leads them towards metamorphosis, like a trail of stones drawing them into the dark forest.

THIS IS A BORZOI BOOK
PUBLISHED BY ALFRED A. KNOPF, INC.
Text copyright © 1990 by Gwen Strauss. Illustrations
copyright © 1990 by Anthony Browne. All rights
reserved under International and Pan-American
Copyright Conventions. Published in the United
States by Alfred A. Knopf, Inc., New York. Distrib-
uted by Random House, Inc., New York. Originally
published in Great Britain by Julia MacRae Books, a
division of Walker Books Ltd., London. Manufac-
tured in Great Britain.

2   4   6   8   0   9   7   5   3   1

LIBRARY OF CONGRESS
CATALOGING-IN-PUBLICATION DATA
Strauss, Gwenn. Trail of stones : poems / by Gwen
Strauss : with drawings by Anthony Browne.   p.
cm. Summary: As they enter the dark wood, familiar
fairy tale characters confront the issues of fear, love,
shame, grief, jealousy, loneliness, and joy in this illus-
trated collection of poems.   ISBN 0-679-80582-6
ISBN 0-679-90582-0 (lib. bdg.)   [1. Fairy tales—
Poetry. 2. Folklore—Poetry. 3. American poetry] I.
Browne, Anthony, ill. II. Title   PS3569.T69225T7
1990   811'.54—dc20   89-38358

# CONTENTS

# THEIR FATHER

I won't say it wasn't my idea.
I think of Hansel's first attempt,
pockets dribbling those white stones,
a tenuous trail to the home
that had ceased to hold him.
I was alone with two children
at the edge of a great wood.

Like that a man can be a fool
when it comes to a woman.
She used to beg for love-making.
Her anger was more
than I had courage for;
her eyes, soft beneath me,
could turn in a frenzy.

When they returned,
following the moon-pebbled path
I vowed never. There are stones
in my belly; they rattle
in my dreams.

The next time Gretel held my hand.
Hansel held back to watch
a cat on the roof. If I'd known
of his scant offerings,
could I have left them?

The time they were away is silent
but for the sawing of inward anger.
I dreamed of birds,
swooping down on their trail.
My wife ate and ate
but grew thin in front of me.

I did nothing. When she died
I drew inside the cottage,
shutters closed, a cage.
I lived in the smallest gestures:
sweeping, building a fire.
I moved as little as possible.

3

If I had the courage
I would enter the woods,
but I clung to cupboard habits.

Gretel, with her apron full of pearls,
has bought us a flock of geese.
Each morning I scatter crumbs for them;
Gretel likes it when I help:
either that, she says, or when I stay
out of her way.

# CONFESSIONS OF A WITCH

No spell works the same way twice.
The need grows deeper, so does the cost.

Whose fist foretold this,
was it in her white palm or mine,
the long heart line to the Mound of Jupiter,
the jealous trail that seeks perfection?

I watched her grow
and watched him.
I was, after all, a woman
in my prime, with kitchen-sink potions:
agrimony, parsley, feverfew—
to seduce, start storms,
clear the fog in the mirror.

She could have lived like a Princess
never dissatisfied with her King—
my King.
The hapless wart placed on some fool's
nose is not enough for me.

I deserved more.
My hunter had the simple task
to have done with her white
hands, rosy cheeks
I'll not be betrayed of my meal,
salted liver and lung.

What a silly fool,
she tried to hide with those
half-men, not even herself
half a woman, but enough
for vanity, that great flaw.
I plied her with corsets, combs,
the apple.

I cannot be contained,
though I will make no excuse;
should I now begin to list
reasons for the magic

he always said was bent?
These bits of me disperse.
I shall not tell what I did
with the apple, that bitter-sweet release.

These years,
hardly a day passed I didn't think
of her, her youthful body,
her white slumber. I kept
to my alchemist's search
in the seven stars, with the seven stones:
I will stop time.

And now, some fool-Prince's found
her with those thumb-sized creatures.

I kept my shape.
Just last week, the eyes of a palace guard,
I caught following me, had to be torn
asunder with a cormorant's claw.

She's changed these years.
Will she know me?

Mirror, I'll not be
outdone by her young Prince—

# THE SEVENTH DWARF

The first night she came
I slept an hour with each
of the others in turn.

She was small boned,
delicate like a dove.
I used to watch the
white of her
arching neck
and black hair
as she swept about
the tables and chairs.
I think she was happy;
we came to like the thought
of her there when we
returned home each day.

Why couldn't she heed
our warnings?
Time and again
we told her to stay
inside the house,
to do her tasks
away from the door.
We urged her daily,
but she was
a flitting butterfly.

The first time
scared me most.
I was stunned
by the stillness
of her white arms.

When the corset
loosened
and she drew that
breath, doubt and joy
washed through us all.

The comb angered me.
What need did she have of combs,
her black hair beautiful

and perfect unhindered?
She was driven by
something—
Perhaps I knew
she would never stay.

So when at last
we returned to her
coma slumber,
I hardly was surprised.
We built a glass casket tomb
to the wonder of the under world
she wandered through.
Kept our solitary vigil.
No one came but three:
the owl, the raven, and the dove.

Yet still in sleep she grew.
We could not contain her.
Nights when I kept watch
I felt something,
as if one could feel the pulse
of a cocoon gripped tightly
in the palm.

He's come
and our life's returned
to the simple cycle
of work and sleep.
Except sometimes I dream
of blood on snow and
then I see her
black hair
falling, arching
across her neck.

# THE PRINCE

Imagine this: we're in the garden harvesting,
and you're telling me how our children suckled,
*Their mouths opened like dark moons.*

When you speak to me like this,
I want you to say everything,
and I want to put my hands on your lips
while you say it.

For a long time I was blind,
even before the thorns of roses tattered my eyes.
I was bored, handsome, a Prince.
The thrill was in what I could get away with.

For the entanglement of arms, legs, hair, I called out,
*Rapunzel,* like a hammer and a saw.
Now I say your name over and over,
a deep humming river. I am an old man in love,

which is not the same thing as a young Prince
adventuring. After I fell from your tower
I wandered through tangled forests,
through the scramble of first frost,
then snow, then false spring. I had changed
and could not return to my father's kingdom.

Imagine this: in the dark, I see your body
with my hands; the soft slack skin of your belly,
the blue hollow behind your ears, your boyish
cropped hair. For days we smile silly.
Sometimes I catch you smiling like that to the spinach.

All my childhood I heard about love
but I thought only witches could grow it
in gardens behind walls too high to climb.

I travelled through blindness
like doubt, with its huge devouring mouth.
The kiss of fern brushed my ankles.
The loamy smell of mushrooms and loss
clung to my fingers. I learned how to cry.

And then you were there,
washing clear my thorn-scratched eyes.
Our skin touching is soft, a baby.
If I were to ask how you grew a garden
in this wasteland, you would say,
*A river of tears and a desert's patience.*

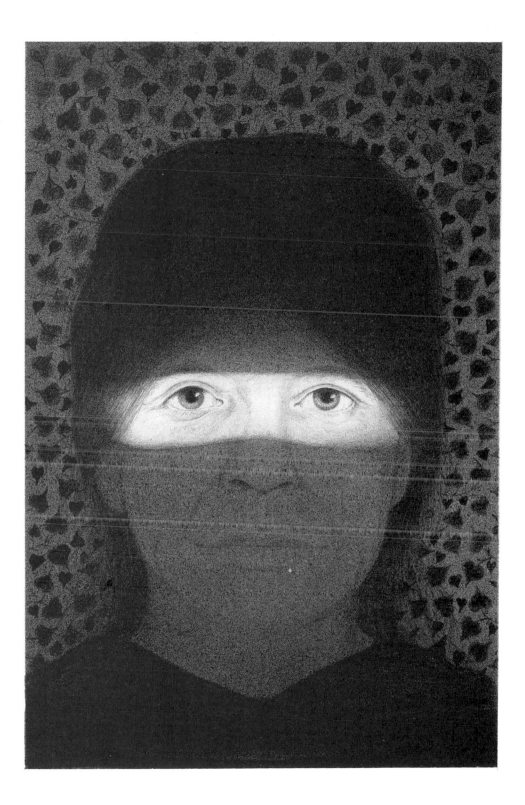

13

# THE WAITING WOLF

First, I saw her feet—
beneath a red pointed cloak
head bent forward
parting the woods,
one foot placed straight
in front of the other.

Then, came her scent.
I was meant to stalk her
smooth, not a twig snaps.
It is the only way I know;
I showed her flowers—
white dead-nettle, nightshade,
devil's bit, wood anemone.

I might not have gone further,
but then nothing ever remains
innocent in the woods.

When she told me about Grandmother,
I sickened. She placed herself on my path,
practically spilling her basket of breads and jams.

Waiting in this old lady's ruffled bed,
I am all calculation. I have gone this far—
dressed in Grandmother's lace panties,
flannel nightgown and cap,
puffs of breath beneath the sheet
lift and fall. I can see my heart tick.
Slightly. Slightly.

These are small lies for a wolf,
but strangely heavy in my belly like stones.
I will forget them as soon as I have her,
still, at this moment I do not like myself.

When she crawls into Grandma's bed,
will she pull me close, thinking:
*This is my grandmother whom I love?*

She will have the youngest skin
I have ever touched, her fingers unfurling
like fiddle heads in spring.

My matted fur will smell to her of forest
moss at night. She'll wonder about my ears,
large, pointed, soft as felt,
my eyes red as her cloak,
my leather nose on her belly.

But perhaps she has known who I am since the first,
since we took the other path
through the woods.

# CINDERELLA

My step-sisters are willing
to cut off their toes for him.

What would I do for those days
when I played alone
in the hazel tree over my mother's grave?

I would go backwards if I could
and stay in that moment when the doves
fluttered down with the golden gown.

But everything has changed.
I trace his form in the ashes,
and then sweep it away before they see.

He's been on parade with that shoe.
All Prince, with heralds and entourage,
they come trumpeting through the village.

If he found me, would he recognize me,
my face, after mistaking their feet for mine?
I want to crawl away

into my pigeon house, my pear tree.
The world is too large, bright like a ballroom
and then suddenly dark.

Mother, no one prepared me for this—
for the soft heat of a man's neck when he dances
or the thickness of his arms.

19

## BLUEBEARD

Come, love, and show me
the small key to my turret-chamber.
Yesterday, in a far off place,
I heard a door scrape a threshold
and the cold clank of metal on stone.

Today, I am returned.
And what, my bride, is this? A stain?
Blood? Again betrayal.

When you arrived in my castle yard,
a country virgin dressed in Paris silks,
I opened all rooms to you but that one,
trusted you with my keys to leave untouched
the one dark corner where I go alone.

Each woman I destroyed, I loved
with infinite tenderness.
Each woman gave herself complete
to me in death, because, as you will find,
there is no freedom greater.

Pain and pleasure are but a moment to either.
Remember this.
Remember our wedding night. In the end,
I will leave no part of you untouched.

In that far place, remember me,
how I remain a prisoner of a little room,
searching for one who loves me as I love.

21

## FOX-WOMAN

Gradually, those prowling nights
will over-grow my other life.
Though only one night a month,
my widowed body lies dead
in our four-posted marriage bed.

There are things
I can not do again: chat with wives
in their gardens, waltz with my older brothers
as other men look on, eat chicken
with forks and knives.

Branches in winter claw at the sky.
The moon circles back.
I dream of walking to church barefoot,
wrapped in a fleece, my face smeared
with blood and lanolin. The villagers stare.

I rattle through days of being human,
with the faint smell of the full moon
and a choked howl.
I have the strangest appetites.
I notice my feet no longer make a sound.

They never trusted my red hair.
When the miller shot my paw,
those stupid villagers looked
sideways. "What's wrong with your hand,
young widow? Why the bandage?"

"Can I make you a poultice?"
They invite me to their dances.
But when the fox circles our village like flame,
they ask, "Didn't you hear the dogs last night?
They came home smelling of her."

The Baker holds two back, straining at their collars.
He apologizes. You can see it in their eyes,
still crazed from last night. It's been said,
the smell of blood can send them
to a frenzy. Sometimes they stay wild

and you have to shoot them.

## THE FROG PRINCESS

I always hated them,
all jump and slime.
The boy next door used to frighten me
with them behind the pool, his palms
cupping something wet and green.

Years later he said he did it all for love;
but I was a Princess then,
wanting nothing more to do with him.
So I wasn't myself
when I made that promise.

I was playing in the garden with my golden ball
Father brought back from his Crusades.
There is a deep well
I sometimes call my name down
to listen to the echo back
and back until I, too, feel hollow.

When I lost my ball, one of them,
bumpy, all eyes and mouth,
heard me or my tears shudder back.
What could I do? I was only a girl,
a Princess, but a girl — so I promised.

It arrived at dinner
lurching its way towards me.
I ordered a halt to its charade,
how dare a frog behave this way.
That's when Father betrayed me.

The meal was endless.
The slurping, burping, warty fellow
drank my royal nectar.

I thought only of escape
to my chamber, my mirror, my bed.
Then the final insult came:
the thing announced it would sleep
with me upon my goose down pillow
and Father nodded, with a distant look.

Three weeks
the puffed up thing
slept beside me.
I dared not move
or even breathe.
In the dark, I watched it
pant, a hollow smudge
on my pillow.

At last I slept and when I woke
my hand touched him.
Shock, then rage
got me hurling him
towards a wall; that's how I got
my Prince to explode from a frog.

# HER SHADOW

Straw burning into gold
smells of rotten eggs
with a hint of lemons and almonds.

Those trinkets—
my mother's wedding ring, her necklace,
they were gifts from my father.
I gave them to him as easily
as my father had given me,
one day on the way to market, boasting.

I would have done anything
for his company in the heaps of straw,
his pimpled face, his songs. I liked his size,
and even his ugliness. We played puns
and riddles while he spun. When he asked
for my child, what did I care for the King's child?

I didn't know then how a baby
can have nothing to do with the father
when it falls asleep in your arms
smelling of sweet-sour milk.

When he came again,
I had not forgotten our time
in the dim room of wheels,
how he woke me with the tender tickling
of straw behind my ears.
The King has never touched me that way.

But I was ashamed and it was easier to despise him.
On the third day he arrived smelling faintly of beer
and baking bread, jovial, less lonely.
He gave back the ring. Then I said his name
and he pulled one leg until he split apart, in front of us.
Since then, I have felt old.

He tore himself in two, for me,
like a shadow, asking for my golden-haired child,
the seed of another man.

## THE BEAST

She left and winter has arrived;
the garden walls grown slick black ice.
I think of how I spied on her while she ate,
how I designed the menu
so she would struggle with her delicacy:
Asian noodles, escargot, partridge that clung
to the bone, lobster she had to peel
from the gaudy red shell.
When she unfurled the white inside, dipped
the soft meat into butter, and let it
dissolve in her pink mouth,
she could have been devouring my heart.

She sends notes:
charming dinner at Lady Belworth's
with father and sisters.
She wore the satin décolleté gown I gave her,
bare white shoulders, neck arched innocently as crocus.
She doesn't mention her plans to return.

The Count Esmire is my able escort, she writes,
so don't fret. Does he slip his handsome arm
beneath her elbow when she steps
onto the cobblestones of a distant city?
Loneliness pulls a tourniquet round my heart,
and I would rend the Count to pieces.

She sent a box of chocolates.
She sends them out of pity.
I feel as small as her smallest daily thought.

This morning's note:
My sisters need me a while longer,
dashed off in her quick pen.
I am a regret, a promise she can't keep.

I crawl on all fours.
I've dug up her rose bushes.
I'm sucking their ivory frozen roots.
I sleep in a pile of rotting mulch. She never comes.

Licking the ice in the fountain
I noticed I'm growing a tail, white, like her roses,

moth wings, snow, the colour of horror
on her face whenever I touched her.

The beast heart survives, waits, and grows uglier.
This morning I know, she is not coming back.

The heart is the last organ to die.
The heart waits. The heart eats away at anything.
The heart builds a prison. My heart mocks me,
beating a sound like her footsteps,
drawing near.

## SLEEPING

For one hundred years, I never dreamed.
I lay at the bottom of a pool, looking up
through salt-green water to the rippled surface
where my mother and father waved.

My mother's tears dripped and made circles
that started small and swelled like pregnancy.
Their crowns flashed and snagged like fish hooks.
When I cried for them only bubbles,
silver balloons wobbled out, silent.

I had visions; they sunk down from the surface
of my past life. Images flickered—
twelve gnarled witches weaving furiously,
a golden plate spun like a top.
It almost sliced my heart.

I willed the rose briar hedge to grow
because I couldn't bear all those princes
blushing, kissing, fumbling with my body.
But still they battled my snarled fence,
their bodies blooming on thorns,
flags, bright as rags of blood.

I wanted instead a room, my pain,
the pin prick, and time alone,
so I stopped watching.
I became a small watery thing
holding my knees and keening.

I had spun my cocoon
of water and blood and there I slept
until my fear wore itself smooth as an eyelid,
as anything that's lived in an ocean.

When I woke to his caress,
I'd grown gold serpent coiled hair.
Now, I fall asleep to the surf of his breath.

When we awaken from our dream,
we feed each other the insides
of yawning blue mussel shells
like kisses, pearled tongues, pried open.